WILDFIRES

Why They Are Increasing and How We Can Adapt

Carla Mooney

San Diego, CA

Printed in the United States

For more information, contact:
ReferencePoint Press, Inc.
PO Box 27779
San Diego, CA 92198
www.ReferencePointPress.com

LIBRARY OF CONGRESS CATALOGING-IN-PUBLICATION DATA

Names: Mooney, Carla, 1970- author
Title: Wildfires : why they are increasing and how we can adapt / by Carla Mooney.
Description: San Diego, CA : ReferencePoint Press, Inc., 2026. | Includes bibliographical references and index.
Identifiers: LCCN 2025029642 (print) | LCCN 2025029643 (ebook) | ISBN 9781678212568 library binding | ISBN 9781678212575 ebook
Subjects: LCSH: Wildfires--Juvenile literature
Classification: LCC SD421.23 .M66 2026 (print) | LCC SD421.23 (ebook) | DDC 363.37/9--dc23/eng/20250902
LC record available at https://lccn.loc.gov/2025029642
LC ebook record available at https://lccn.loc.gov/2025029643

CONTENTS

Historic Devastation

In early 2025 wildfires burned across Southern California. Intense flames spread rapidly and destroyed homes and buildings, displaced thousands of people, and filled the skies with thick smoke. Entire communities were evacuated as firefighters battled for weeks to gain control of the dangerous blazes.

Hiking guide Amanda Getty was one of the thousands of Californians forced to evacuate their homes as the fires raged. Getty, who lives in Pasadena with her husband and daughter, became concerned when nearby Eaton Canyon caught fire in early January 2025. Her husband was out of town, and Getty wondered whether she should evacuate with her daughter. At first she decided to wait for guidance from officials. She put her daughter to bed and fell asleep reading coverage of the fires on social media. At 3:30 a.m., Getty woke to her phone buzzing from a neighbor's text. It was time to go. Within minutes, police cars drove through her neighborhood, blaring sirens and warning residents of the approaching flames. Getty grabbed her daughter and dog and ran for her car. "The wind was trying to knock us over as we ran,"[1] she says. Getty and her daughter made it to safety.

When Getty and her husband returned to their neighborhood the next day, they saw that many of their neighbors' homes had burned. Their home was still standing, but it had sustained significant smoke damage. The couple worked to clear brush from their property and spray the roof with water to prevent sparks in the air from igniting it.

Many other Californians were not as lucky. Dale Fielder and his wife Patricia evacuated their burning Altadena home early on January 8. Dale returned to his neighborhood the next day and saw the devastation of the wildfire. "I get to my block . . . and I could not believe it," he says. "Not a single house was standing, and I'll never forget that as long as I live. . . . And finally, I pull up in front of my house, and just—it was smoldering. It was gone. And that's when I just sat in that car. I couldn't move. And I, for 15, 20 minutes, I just cry. I bellowed."[2] The Fielders had lost everything.

California has always been vulnerable to wildfires because of its hot, dry summers and strong winds. But in 2025 wildfires reached a new level of destruction. Wildfires burned over 50,000 acres (20,234 ha), destroyed thousands of buildings, caused billions of dollars in damage, and killed about thirty people. Residents of suburban neighborhoods suddenly found themselves being ordered to evacuate. Entire neighborhoods burned to the ground. Schools closed, electrical power grids were shut down,

The Eaton fire burns in Los Angeles in 2025. The fire destroyed thousands of buildings and caused billions of dollars in damage.

and emergency shelters filled with people seeking safety from the fires. In an interview, California governor Gavin Newsom said that he believed the January 2025 wildfires in the greater Los Angeles area were one of the worst natural disasters in US history. "I think it will be in terms of just the costs associated with it, in terms of the scale and scope,"[3] Newsom said in a January 2025 interview.

A Global Threat

California is not alone in dealing with wildfires. Wildfires are becoming a growing problem around the world. They are no longer limited to just hot, dry areas. As the earth's climate changes, more regions are experiencing extreme heat, longer droughts, and drier vegetation. These conditions create the perfect environment for wildfires to start and spread. Over the past several years, wildfires have become more frequent, destructive, and deadly. They are burning in areas where they were previously rare. And fire season, the time of year when fires are most likely to start and spread, has grown longer.

The global threat of wildfires hit hard in 2023, when wildfires devastated numerous countries, including Canada and Greece. In Canada 2023 was the most destructive wildfire season in the country's history. Over six thousand fires burned 37 million acres (15 million ha) of land, an area bigger than England. The 2023 fires were widespread, breaking out from Canada's West Coast to its Atlantic provinces. Smoke from the fires spread across North America, turning skies orange in cities as far away as New York and Washington, DC. The air quality reached dangerous levels, and health officials instructed millions of people to stay indoors.

Greece also faced devastating wildfires in 2023. During one of the hottest summers on record, wildfires burned through forests, farmlands, and small villages. Fires threatened ancient Greek ruins and wildlife habitats as tourists and residents were evacuated from the fire's path. Over 345,950 acres (140,000 ha) burned, hundreds of structures were destroyed, and more than twenty people died.

An Increasing Concern

Wildfires threaten human health, property, and the environment. The danger is increasing worldwide as wildfires burn more frequently, more intensely, and in more places. Flames destroy homes, ruin farmlands, and devastate communities. Smoke from wildfires travels through the atmosphere, harming people's health thousands of miles away. Wildfires scorch forests and wipe out important habitats for animals and plants. Burning forests also release heat-trapping greenhouse gases into the atmosphere, making the earth warmer and creating dry, warm conditions ideal for more fires.

> **"As communities in the U.S. and around the world suffer increasingly devastating damages from wildfires and wildfire smoke, it is becoming more and more obvious that we must dramatically change our ways of living to reduce risk."[4]**
>
> —Paige Fischer, principal investigator of the Western Forest and Fire Initiative at the University of Michigan

In response, communities worldwide must adapt and take action to protect lives and property. Paige Fischer, principal investigator of the Western Forest and Fire Initiative at the University of Michigan, makes this point when she says, "As communities in the U.S. and around the world suffer increasingly devastating damages from wildfires and wildfire smoke, it is becoming more and more obvious that we must dramatically change our ways of living to reduce risk."[4]

CHAPTER ONE

What Are Wildfires?

On August 8, 2023, a spark from a broken power line on the Hawaiian island of Maui ignited a nearby patch of dry vegetation. Winds from a nearby hurricane quickly fanned the small fire into a deadly wildfire. The high winds carried burning embers to dry grassland areas, where flames erupted. The fire continued to grow and spread in minutes, overwhelming the town of Lahaina and reaching the island's Pacific coast in an astoundingly short time. "We saw spot fires at the oceanfront within an hour, within about 90 minutes," says Steve Kerber, vice president and executive director of the Fire Safety Research Institute, which issued a 2024 fact-finding report on the Maui fire. "So, traveling over a mile within about 90 minutes is incredibly fast."[5]

The speed and size of the Maui fire caught many Lahaina residents off guard. Flames, downed utility poles, and electrical lines blocked several evacuation routes. In desperation, some people went into the ocean to escape the fire. John Singer attempted to save his home as the wildfire moved closer to his neighborhood. He climbed onto the roof, used a garden hose to soak his home, and tried to put out flames as they got close. But the fire was too fast and too strong. Singer ran into the ocean to escape the flames. Once he was in the water, Singer looked back at his house. "Devastation—everything gone. There's just nothing left. From the houses to the markets to the businesses, it's like a nuclear bomb went off here. There's nothing left,"[6] Singer says.

The 2023 Maui wildfire was the worst natural disaster in Hawaiian history and the fifth-deadliest wildfire in US history. It destroyed over twenty-two hundred homes and other structures and caused approximately $5.5 billion in damages. The deadly wildfire also claimed the lives of more than one hundred people.

> "Devastation—everything gone. There's just nothing left. From the houses to the markets to the businesses, it's like a nuclear bomb went off here. There's nothing left."[6]
>
> —John Singer, survivor of the 2023 Maui fires

What Are Wildfires?

Wildfires are uncontrolled fires that burn through natural areas like forests, grasslands, prairies, and wetlands. These fires can start with a small spark and quickly grow into massive blazes that cover thousands of acres. Wildfires can burn in vegetation that is above or in the soil. A ground fire usually starts in soil rich with organic matter, such as plant roots. A ground fire can burn slowly for a long time until it grows into a surface fire. A surface fire burns in dry or dead vegetation near the ground. Dry grasses and

The 2023 Maui fire caught many residents off guard. This memorial in Lahaina shows photos of those who died in the fire.

fallen leaves often provide fuel for surface fires. A crown fire burns higher and climbs into the leaves and tops of trees and shrubs.

Wildfires are a natural part of many ecosystems. Some environments depend on wildfires to stay healthy. Fires can help clear out dead plants, allowing new grasses and plants to grow. Fires clean the forest floor, burning debris and returning nutrients to the soil. They thin heavy forest cover, allowing sunlight to reach small plants near the ground and allowing large trees to grow. Wildfires can also kill insects and diseases that harm trees and plants. Wildfires can even help some plants reproduce. For example, some pine cones only open and release their seeds when exposed to heat from a fire. Other plants, including the chamise and scrub oak, need the fire's heat for their seeds to germinate. Some plant species depend on wildfires every few years, while others only need a fire a few times a century to move through their natural life cycle.

While wildfires can be beneficial, they are unpredictable. Wildfires that are too frequent, too intense, and burn too close to human communities can do serious harm. A 2023 study by the US Congress Joint Economic Committee estimated that wildfires cost the United States $394 billion to $893 billion annually. These costs include direct damages to homes and businesses, wildfire suppression and firefighting, and indirect costs such as lost income and tourism. And wildfires can be deadly, injuring and killing people in their path. In 2023, 130 people in the United States died from wildfires, the highest number since 1990.

How Wildfires Start

Every wildfire begins with a spark that sets material on fire. Sparks can come from natural sources or human activity. Lightning is the most common natural cause of wildfires. When lightning strikes trees, shrubs, or dry grass, it can cause flames that ignite the surrounding vegetation. According to the National Interagency Fire Center, more than sixty-one hundred wildfires in the United States were caused by lightning strikes in 2024.

The Wildland-Urban Interface

In recent decades, more people have moved into areas considered to be part of the wildland–urban interface (WUI). The WUI is the region where homes, businesses, and other structures are built near or within forests, shrublands, grasslands, and other wilderness areas. As the US population has increased and housing prices in cities have risen, more people have moved into the WUI. An estimated 33 percent of all US homes were located in the WUI in 2020, according to Resources for the Future. And that amount is expanding. According to the US Fire Administration, the WUI grows by approximately 2 million acres (809,371 ha) annually. In the United States, California, Texas, Florida, North Carolina, and Pennsylvania have the most houses in the WUI. As more people and businesses move into the WUI, their risk from wildfires increases. Homes in the WUI are more likely to be damaged by wildfires because nearby vegetation fuels the fires and allows flames to rapidly spread. Once the fire engulfs one home, it can easily spread from home to home, quickly engulfing entire streets and neighborhoods. Additionally, fighting fires in the WUI can be challenging because dense vegetation and nearby structures make it difficult for firefighters to access and control flames.

The majority of wildfires are caused by human activity. Experts estimate that 85 to 90 percent of wildfires are started by human activity. Many wildfires start by accident. A smoldering campfire, burning backyard trash, sparks from power lines, and even sparks from hot engines can ignite a fire in dry grass or other vegetation. Even something as simple as a glass bottle that focuses and magnifies the sun's rays can ignite a fire on a warm, dry day. A fire only needs the right conditions and a single accidental spark to ignite and burn.

Sometimes, wildfires are set intentionally, a serious crime called arson. More than 20 percent of all human-caused wildfires in the United States are the result of arson, according to the National Interagency Fire Center. In 2024 Ronnie Dean Stout II was arrested and charged with arson in connection with the Park Fire in Northern California. Prosecutors said Stout started the fire by pushing a burning car down a 60-foot (18 m) embankment. Because the region was in the middle of an extreme heat wave, the initial blaze quickly spread across the dry land and burned more than 430,000 acres (174,015 ha). In court, Stout pleaded

When lightning strikes trees, shrubs, or grasses, it can ignite vegetation. Lightning is the main natural cause of wildfires.

innocent to the arson charges and insisted he did not intend to start the massive wildfire. "If they light that fire, regardless of their intent, they have no control of how big it gets,"[7] says Gianni Muschetto, staff chief at the California Department of Forestry and Fire Protection.

Other times, a person does not intend to hurt anyone, but their carelessness leads to a fire. "Human carelessness is the biggest contributing factor to the start of wildfires,"[8] says Joseph Roise, a professor of forestry and environmental resources at North Carolina State University. Unattended campfires, discarded cigarettes, sparks from power tools or machinery, matches, and fireworks can create the initial spark needed to ignite a wildfire. When people burn garbage or other debris in their yards, the wind can spread burning embers to other areas, causing a new fire to spark. Sometimes, people do not completely put out a campfire or other fire,

> **"Human carelessness is the biggest contributing factor to the start of wildfires."[8]**
>
> —Joseph Roise, a professor of forestry and environmental resources at North Carolina State University

and an errant ember that lands in the right conditions can ignite a new fire.

Utilities and electrical equipment can also cause wildfires. Power lines that fall or spark, like the one that caused the 2023 Maui fire, can ignite fires in surrounding vegetation. Electrical equipment malfunctions also cause fires worldwide. Other times, farm and construction equipment emit sparks that can ignite a fire in nearby vegetation. Even sparks from a car can start a fire. For example, the 2018 Carr Fire in California began when a trailer got a flat tire. When its metal wheel rim scraped the road's pavement, it created sparks that started the blaze. The fire quickly spread in hot, dry, windy conditions and burned nearly 230,000 acres (93,078 ha). Several people died, and more than one thousand homes and buildings were destroyed.

How Wildfires Spread

Once a wildfire starts, it can spread extremely fast, sometimes faster than a person can run. The spread of a wildfire depends on three main factors: fuel, weather, and topography. These three factors are known as the fire behavior triangle.

The first part of the fire behavior triangle is fuel. Fires need fuel to burn. A wildfire's fuel can be grass, leaves, shrubs, trees, and buildings. Grasses and small vegetation tend to burn quicker and generate less heat than larger fuel sources such as trees. Areas filled with dry vegetation provide a lot of fuel for wildfires. The more fuel available for the fire to burn, the larger and hotter the fire can grow, and the faster it can spread.

Some plants, shrubs, and trees contain oils and resins that cause them to burn faster and hotter. For example, pine and other conifer trees contain resin and oils in their sap and foliage. The resin and oils are flammable, causing these trees to burn more intensely and produce more embers. Drier vegetation will also burn faster than plants and shrubs with more moisture. For example, oak leaves are often drier than the leaves of

Moisture Content

Moisture content in a fire's fuel is one of the most important factors in how fast a fire spreads, how intense it becomes, and how much smoke it produces. Moisture content is the percentage of moisture in a fuel. Moisture content varies by vegetation type, size, shape, sun exposure, atmospheric conditions, and whether the vegetation is alive or dead. Drier fuels produce longer flame lengths, spread faster, and generate more heat. Some fine fuels, like grass and pine needles, gain and lose moisture quickly as compared to larger fuels such as logs and branches. For example, a period of sunshine after a heavy rain can quickly dry out grass, while logs remain moist inside. The dry grass will burn quickly, but the log retains more moisture and will be less likely to ignite. Dead fuels, such as leaves and sticks, generally have a lower moisture content than live vegetation and will burn more quickly. Living plants with higher moisture content can slow a fire and reduce its spread. Moisture in living plants generally peaks in the early spring, when soil moisture is high and there is more precipitation. At the end of summer, moisture content typically drops to its lowest levels.

other hardwood trees, making them more flammable and likely to spread a wildfire.

The weather has an important role in how fires grow and spread. High temperatures and low humidity dry out plants, shrubs, and trees, creating ideal conditions for a fire to ignite and burn faster. Wildfires typically become the most intense and spread fastest in the afternoon because the air is hottest.

The presence of wind can make a wildfire more dangerous and enable it to spread faster and farther. Wind provides the fire with oxygen, which causes it to grow and spread faster. Wind also carries burning embers to new places. When the embers land on dry vegetation or other flammable material, they can ignite new fires, called spot fires, far from the original wildfire. "If the wind is really strong, you can expect to see a wildfire that's moving quickly," Roise says. "There might even be some embers that spread and start fires in locations that are sometimes up to a quarter of a mile away from the original fire."[9]

Topography, which is the shape of the land, also affects how a wildfire spreads. Wildfires typically move faster uphill than downhill because fire heat rises, dries out the vegetation growing uphill, and causes it to ignite faster. Areas that create a wind tunnel effect, such as canyons, valleys, or mountain slopes, can be particularly dangerous when a wildfire breaks out. The narrow gap between tall sides causes the wind to accelerate and strengthen as it moves through the narrow passage, causing wildfire flames to spread faster.

Firefighters use their knowledge of the fire behavior triangle—fuel, weather, and topography—to predict how fires will grow, where they will move, and how to stop them. However, where there is an abundance of fuel, hot and dry weather, strong winds, and certain types of landscapes, wildfires can quickly become nearly impossible to control.

Where Wildfires Are Most Common

While wildfires can occur anywhere in the world, some areas are more at risk than others due to their geography, climate, and vegetation. In the United States, California, Texas, and North Carolina regularly experience high numbers of wildfires.

In 2023 more than seventy-three hundred wildfires burned over 330,000 acres (133,546 ha) in California. The state typically experiences very dry, hot summers, which dry out vegetation. California also experiences strong wind gusts that can spread wildfires quickly. Many California communities have been built near forests, rangeland, or other wild vegetation. These communities face a higher risk of wildfires since the fires can easily spread from the wild areas to neighborhoods, causing property damage and forcing evacuations.

One of the deadliest wildfires in California history burned in 2018. The Camp Fire began near the town of Paradise in Northern California. A faulty electric power line emitted sparks that ignited nearby dry grass. High winds drove the fire to spread with incredible speed. "The tinder-dry vegetation and Red Flag conditions consisting of strong winds, low humidity,

> "The tinder-dry vegetation and Red Flag conditions consisting of strong winds, low humidity, and warm temperatures promoted this fire and caused extreme rates of spread."[10]
>
> —CAL FIRE, the statewide firefighting and resource management agency

and warm temperatures promoted this fire and caused extreme rates of spread,"[10] according to CAL FIRE, the statewide firefighting and resource management agency. The deadly Camp Fire killed eighty-five people and destroyed more than 18,800 structures. The town of Paradise was almost completely destroyed.

In Texas approximately seventy-one hundred wildfires ignited in 2023, burning more than 210,000 acres (84,984 ha). The state's vast grasslands and dry brush provide ideal fuel for wildfires. Most of Texas's fires burn in the spring and summer, when conditions are the hottest and driest. Ranching and farming activities in the state also increase the risk of accidental fires.

In the US South, North Carolina experiences hundreds of wildfires annually. In 2023, 5,214 fires burned across nearly 74,000 acres (29,947 ha). Many of North Carolina's wildfires start in the state's coastal plains. In these areas, the soil is rich with peat, an accumulation of partially decayed organic matter. Dry peat is extremely flammable, and peat-rich soils can burn underground for weeks. North Carolina's pine forests and dry leaves also provide ideal fuel for wildfires.

Increasing Wildfire Activity

Wildfires have always been unpredictable and dangerous. However, in recent years, wildfire activity has increased. There are more wildfires each year, and they are getting bigger. Fires that once burned a few hundred acres now burn thousands. In the 1980s US wildfires burned less than 3 million acres (1.2 million ha) in most years, according to the National Interagency Fire Center. In 2024 alone, wildfires burned nearly 9 million acres (3.6 million ha) in the United States. Many fires have become megafires, burning more than 100,000 acres (40,469 ha). Firefighters spend weeks controlling these megafires, often bringing in firefighting teams from other regions to help.

Wildfires are also growing more severe. Extreme wildfires burn hotter, spread faster, and are harder to control and contain. Scientists from the National Aeronautics and Space Administration studied satellite data over a twenty-one-year period and found that extreme wildfires have doubled worldwide. Extreme wildfires have become more frequent, more intense, and larger. The scientists found that the biggest increase in extreme wildfires occurred in the western United States' conifer forests and the boreal forests of Northern Russia and North America. The scientists believe that warmer nighttime temperatures are driving the increase in extreme wildfire activity, since these higher temperatures allow fires to keep burning overnight.

US Wildfires Are Growing in Size and Intensity

Data compiled by the National Interagency Fire Center for the period between 1983 and 2024 reveals that the number of wildfires occurring in the United States during those years has been relatively steady. What has changed is the size and intensity of those fires. Land area burned has dramatically increased as wildfires have become larger and more intense.

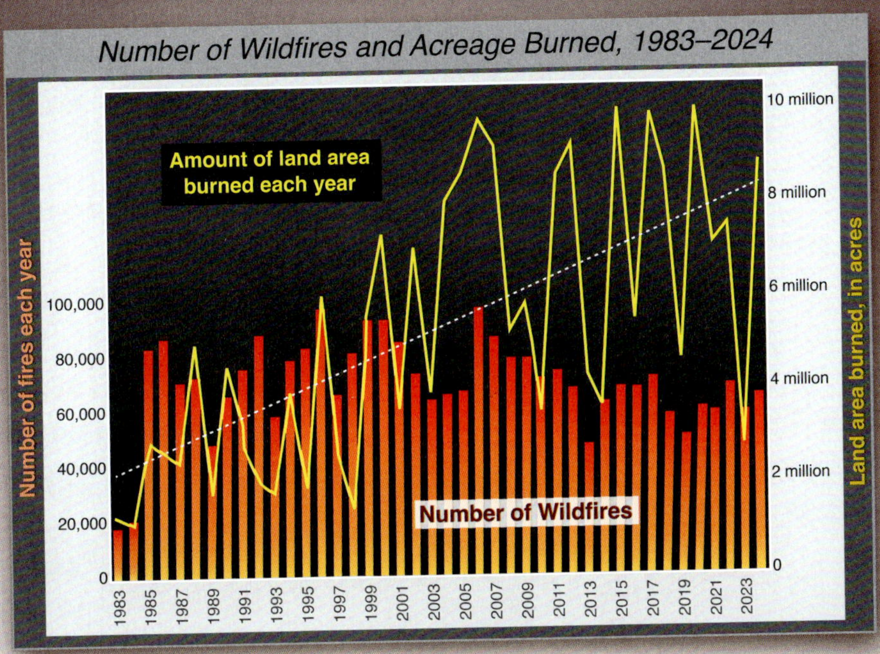

Source: "Wildfires and Climate Change," NASA, May 28, 2025. https://science.nasa.gov/.

In regions worldwide, fire season—the period when the risk of wildfires is highest—is also growing longer. In past years, the US fire season ran for about five months, from late spring to early fall. Now, the US fire season in many states has extended to seven months, from May to November. Warmer temperatures and drier conditions have made it easier for fires to start and spread almost year-round. In December 2021 the Marshall Fire in Colorado spread quickly when strong winds whipped grass and brush fires near the city of Boulder and pushed the fires toward the nearby towns of Superior and Louisville. The high winds carried burning embers into neighborhoods, setting homes, trees, and other structures on fire. By the time it was contained, the Marshall Fire destroyed or damaged nearly eleven hundred homes and displaced thousands of people.

Wildfires have burned throughout the earth's history. In some situations, wildfires can benefit the environment, clearing out dead plants, cleaning the forest floor, and killing harmful insects and disease. However, wildfires can quickly grow out of control. When they do, they threaten communities, property, and lives.

CHAPTER TWO

Why Are Wildfires Increasing?

Wildfires are happening more often and burning larger areas than ever before. They are also becoming more intense and destructive, threatening homes, forests, animals, and human lives. In many parts of the world, especially in the western United States, wildfires have become a normal part of life during certain times of the year.

Scientists and firefighters agree that the rise in wildfires worldwide does not have a single cause. Instead, several factors are driving the increase in wildfires, including climate change, human activity, forest management practices, and environmental changes. Together, these factors have created ideal conditions for fires to burn more often, be more intense, and cause significant damage to communities worldwide.

Climate Change

One of the biggest factors driving the increase in wildfires is climate change. Climate is the usual weather or weather pattern of a region and can vary depending on location. Climate change occurs when a region's usual weather patterns change over time. These changes can include variations in average temperatures, the amount of rainfall, and the intensity of storms in the area. Unlike the weather, which can change daily, climate change is much slower and occurs over hundreds or thousands of years.

> "A hotter season paired with drier vegetation can lead to more wildfires that are harder to contain."[11]
>
> —Kai Chen, director of research at the Yale Center on Climate Change and Health

Many factors can cause climate change. In the past, the earth's climate changed because of natural occurrences unrelated to human activity, such as changes in the earth's orbit, volcanic eruptions, or landform shifts. However, most scientists agree that the earth's current warming trend is not a natural event. Instead, they believe human activity is the leading cause of modern climate change. Human activities, especially burning fossil fuels, have caused the earth's climate to change at its current rapid rate. The earth is getting warmer, and that has a direct effect on how often wildfires occur and how severe they become.

The effects of climate change—such as warmer temperatures, lower precipitation levels, and increasing drought patterns—all contribute to making wildfires more dangerous. "A hotter season paired with drier vegetation can lead to more wildfires that are harder to contain. Stronger winds also add more oxygen to fires, allowing them to spread even faster,"[11] says Kai Chen, director of research at the Yale Center on Climate Change and Health.

> "As climate change worsens, so too does the risk of ever larger and more severe wildfires."[12]
>
> —Jonathan Overpeck, dean of the School for Environment and Sustainability at the University of Michigan

As the earth continues to warm, climate experts predict that wildfire risk will also increase. Writing in 2025, Jonathan Overpeck, dean of the School for Environment and Sustainability at the University of Michigan, states, "The current North American wildfire season is surging across the western U.S. and Canada, made worse by the warming and drying effects of human-caused climate change. As climate change worsens, so too does the risk of ever larger and more severe wildfires."[12]

Rising Temperatures and Drier Conditions

As the earth's climate warms, many regions are experiencing hotter and drier weather. These dry conditions make it easier for fires to start and spread. Trees, grasses, and other plants lose mois-

A dried-up riverbed in Montana. In recent years, many parts of the western United States have experienced drought conditions, and this makes it easier for fires to start and to spread.

ture and become like dry kindling, which is perfect fuel for a fire. "Coupled with longer periods of time that are hotter and drier, we have all of this vegetation rapidly drying out, increasing the probability of ignition. Once those materials ignite, they often create large wildfires that are difficult to suppress,"[13] says Adam Coates, a Virginia Tech fire ecology and management expert.

Even a small increase in temperature can lead to a much larger area being burned by wildfires. According to the Center for Climate and Energy Solutions, an average annual temperature increase of only one degree Celsius would cause the average burned area to expand by as much as 600 percent in parts of the US West.

Longer Droughts and Early Snowmelt

Droughts are part of the earth's natural climate cycles, but climate change is altering their usual patterns. A drought occurs when an area receives less rain or snow than it usually receives over a year. Without needed rain or snow, plants and soil dry up, and

Global Warming

Human activity is a significant factor in the earth's warming temperatures. The earth's atmosphere is made up of a layer of gases, called greenhouse gases, that surrounds the planet and acts like a blanket that absorbs the sun's heat and keeps the earth warm. This process enables the earth's temperature to stay relatively steady. Humans have been burning fossil fuels such as coal, oil, and natural gas for energy at an increasing rate since the Industrial Revolution in the 1700s and 1800s. While burning fossil fuels generates energy, it also releases more greenhouse gases, including carbon dioxide, into the atmosphere. As more greenhouse gases build up in the atmosphere, more heat is released by the earth's surface, which is absorbed and then radiated back to the earth, increasing the planet's surface temperature.

the water stored in wetlands, lakes, and rivers decreases. Water stored in the soil and underground in aquifers also declines.

Because of climate change, droughts are becoming more common, longer, and more intense. Many parts of the western United States have experienced drought conditions since 2000. The twenty-two-year period from 2000 to 2022 was the driest in the western United States since at least 800 CE, according to a 2022 report by Nature Climate Change.

Climate change is also altering how droughts develop. Historically, droughts occur because of a lack of rain or precipitation. However, the current drought in the US West is instead being driven by higher temperatures. Scientists from the University of California, Los Angeles (UCLA), the National Oceanic and Atmospheric Administration (NOAA), and the Cooperative Institute for Research in Environmental Sciences partnered to study the historic US West drought. Their 2024 study found that higher temperatures, instead of reduced rainfall, were the main driver of the drought's increasing severity. The scientists predict that as the earth's climate warms, droughts will last longer, impact more regions, and become more severe. "For generations, drought has been associated with drier than normal weather," says Veva Deheza, director of NOAA's National Integrated Drought Information System and study coauthor. "This study further confirms we've entered a new paradigm where rising temperatures are leading to intense droughts with precipitation as a secondary factor."[14]

Climate change and warming temperatures also impact the snowpack in mountain regions. A snowpack is a seasonal accumulation of snow that remains on the ground throughout the winter and gradually melts during the warmer months. Snowpack acts as a natural water reservoir, and as it gradually melts in the spring and summer, it provides water for streams, reservoirs, and groundwater aquifers. Snowmelt also serves as a natural fire retardant. When snowpack melts slowly in the spring, the flow of water keeps the ground and nearby vegetation moist. Warmer temperatures mean that less precipitation falls as snow, reducing the amount of snowpack. Warmer temperatures also cause snowpack to melt earlier in the year. When peak fire season arrives in the summer, the snowmelt is long gone, and everything is dry.

Increase in Lightning Strikes

Lightning is the most common natural cause of wildfires, triggering dry vegetation to ignite into flames. For example, in August 2020 a storm caused approximately fifteen thousand lightning strikes in central and Northern California over a few days. The lightning ignited more than six hundred fires in the state, which burned over 2 million acres (809,371 ha).

Climate scientists have discovered that the earth's warming temperatures may lead to more thunderstorms, especially dry ones. Dry thunderstorms produce lightning but little rain. More lightning means more chances for wildfires to ignite, especially in areas where the vegetation is already dry. A 2022 study published by Washington State University scientists found that dry lightning, which occurs when there is lightning with less than 2.5 millimeters of rainfall, has become a significant cause of some of the biggest wildfires in California. As climate change makes the likelihood of dry conditions and lightning more common, the risk of lightning-sparked wildfires will also likely increase.

Wildfires are becoming more intense and burning larger areas than ever before.

Atmospheric scientist David Romps, director of the Berkeley Atmospheric Sciences Center, agrees that climate change will cause more high-risk lightning strikes. "The evidence from looking at climate models is that we can expect that lightning will increase. My best guess is that by the end of the century, if we continue to burn coal and fossil fuels, we anticipate an increase of the number of lightning strikes by 50%,"[15] says Romps.

Human Activity

Climate change creates hotter, drier conditions that make it easier for wildfires to start and spread. While natural causes such as lightning can ignite fires, most of the time human activity has a major role in starting wildfires. Scientists estimate that up to 90 percent of wildfires are started by human activity.

As towns and cities grow, more people are building homes in the wildland–urban interface, the area where human development meets undeveloped land. These areas are typically filled with trees, bushes, and other vegetation, which can provide an ideal fuel for wildfires if ignited. The closer people live to these areas, the greater the chance of human activity starting a fire.

> "If ninety percent of fires are started by human beings, and our population is growing, and people are expanding out into more rural areas or going and recreating in natural areas more often, it's just a matter of time before statistically you're going to start seeing more and more fires start."[16]
>
> —Terry Baker, chief executive officer of the Society of American Foresters

Once a fire ignites and begins to burn, the proximity of homes and buildings makes it more likely that the fire will threaten property and lives. "If ninety percent of fires are started by human beings, and our population is growing, and people are expanding out into more rural areas or going and recreating in natural areas more often, it's just a matter of time before statistically you're going to start seeing more and more fires start,"[16] says Terry Baker, chief executive officer of the Society of American Foresters.

Forest Management Practices

In nature, small fires actually help keep forests healthy. Indigenous communities practiced controlled burning to manage the land and reduce fire risk. These low-intensity fires burned away dry grass, dead branches, dry leaves, and brush, preventing larger fires later on. They also regularly thinned overgrown forests by removing excess trees and brush to reduce fire risk.

As more people have moved near forests and wildlands, many communities have followed a different approach to forest management. For many years, communities attempted to extinguish wildfires as quickly as possible. This practice protected property and lives, but it also created long-term problems. By putting out every small fire, communities prevented natural, controlled wildfires from clearing dry leaves, dead trees, and underbrush. Over time, this material builds up and becomes additional fuel for fires. When a fire does ignite, the fuel buildup allows it to burn much hotter and faster. As a result, the wildfire becomes more intense, difficult to control, and destructive.

The Spread of Invasive Species

The spread of invasive species also makes wildfires more difficult to control and contain. An invasive species is a plant or animal that is not native to an area and has a negative impact on the environment and the ecosystems of the area. Around the world, invasive grasses are fueling damaging wildfires. "Invasive species can and do play a large role in some wildland fires, contributing both to the total amount of fuel available to burn and in some cases altering the overall flammability of the vegetation,"[17] says Adam Coates.

Invasive plant species impact wildfires in several ways. First, invasive plants, particularly invasive grasses, increase the amount of fuel available for a wildfire to burn. These plants often grow quickly and form dense, dry patches of vegetation that easily ignite and fuel more frequent and intense wildfires. Invasive species also change traditional wildfire patterns by growing in areas that are historically low-risk for wildfires. The arrival of the invasive grass increases the area's wildfire risk. Areas that were rarely threatened by fire in the past are more likely to find themselves in the path of large, dangerous wildfires.

Invasive plants can also displace native plants, creating a destructive loop in which the invasive species fuels fires that burn native plants. The invasive species quickly regrows in burned areas, crowding out native plants that are slower to recover after a fire. As the invasive species takes over, it provides even more fuel for the next fire.

In eastern Oregon, rocky areas of open ground and little vegetation provided a place where firefighters could base operations for decades. The areas had little fuel for wildfires, so they became a barrier that could help stop a spreading fire. However, the introduction of an invasive grass, *Ventenata dubia*, changed everything in 2015. The grass, commonly known as wire grass, created a carpet of dry vegetation that provided a highly flammable fuel for fires. Oregon firefighter Jeff Priest realized fighting fires in Oregon had just gotten much more difficult. "We knew

Flammable Plants

No plant is fireproof. All can ignite under the right conditions. However, some plants are more flammable than others. Plants that contain oils, resins, waxes, or gummy sap ignite quickly. Examples of this type of flammable plant include acacia, bamboo, eucalyptus, Japanese honeysuckle, rosemary, and Scotch broom. Another plant, the gas plant, gets its name from the flammable vapors its leaves and flowers emit. Trees with paperlike bark, such as river birch trees, are more flammable than others. Among trees, cedar, cypress, fir, juniper, pine, and spruce contain resins and saps that easily ignite. These evergreen trees and shrubs also have fine needles that, when dropped to the ground, provide fire fuel. When these flammable plants are invasive in an area, they can spread quickly and crowd out less-flammable native plants.

it was coming. But all of a sudden, it was there,"[18] says Priest about the invasive wire grass. Researchers from Oregon State University studied the impact of wire grass on wildfires in the region. Their results were alarming. The researchers found that areas overtaken by the wire grass had fifty times more fire fuel than areas without the invasive species.

A Worldwide Problem

The northwestern United States is just one region dealing with invasive species that are impacting wildfire risk and behavior. In Brazil molasses grass from Africa has turned large regions of the Cerrado savanna into a high fire-risk grassland. In the western United States, buffel grass fuels fires in the Sonoran Desert that threaten native saguaro cacti, while highly flammable cheatgrass crowds out native sagebrush in the Great Basin. Meanwhile, in the southeastern United States, cogon grass overwhelms native plants and burns at high temperatures, providing more fuel for intense, destructive fires.

Most of these invasive grasses originated in Africa or Europe but have expanded their ranges worldwide. Humans have helped the spread of invasive grasses by scattering grass seeds in new areas, sometimes intentionally to feed livestock or control erosion. "The [grass] invasions in the last 100 years or so are just a radical example of a speeded-up process that's been happening over millennia,"[19] says Dave Richardson, an ecologist and invasive plant expert at South Africa's Stellenbosch University.

Once invasive grasses are established, their impact on wildfires can become a dangerous cycle. These grasses grow quickly and catch fire easily, which helps a fire spread faster and farther. After a fire, invasive grasses like cheatgrass often grow back faster than native species and become even more fuel for the next fire. With each fire, the invasive grasses spread farther.

Invasive Insects

Invasive insect species are also contributing to the increasingly dangerous wildfires. The earth's warming temperatures have allowed some insect species to survive and reproduce in new regions. In some areas, these invasive insects have impacted fire

Bark beetles kill trees, which then become easier fuel for future forest fires. These beetles have infested millions of acres of forests in North America.

behavior and fuel sources. For example, invasive bark beetles have infested millions of acres of forests in North America. These tiny insects bore into trees, killing them. Forests become more vulnerable to wildfire as the dry, dead trees become new fuel for fires. Additionally, when the standing trees ignite, the fire's flames can climb to the treetops and spread quickly from tree to tree through the forest canopy.

Wildfires are increasing in both number and severity due to a combination of natural and human-caused factors. Climate change dries out landscapes and leads to longer, hotter fire seasons. Human activities, both intentional and accidental, spark more fires than ever before. Past forest management decisions have allowed too much fire fuel to build up, while the spread of invasive plants and insect species makes forests and other wildlands more flammable. Together, these factors are driving the increasing threat from wildfires worldwide.

What Are the Consequences of More Frequent, Destructive Wildfires?

Wildfires have always been a part of nature, but in recent years they have become more frequent and destructive than ever before. As temperatures rise, droughts last longer, and forests grow drier, wildfires are burning more land and threatening more lives. Wildfires impact everything around them, destroying wildlife habitats, damaging homes, polluting the air and water, costing billions of dollars, and harming the health and lives of humans and animals. As wildfires increase, the consequences will become a bigger problem for communities worldwide.

Environmental and Ecosystem Impacts

Wildfires significantly impact the environment by altering landscapes, disrupting ecosystems, and releasing pollutants into the air and water. Wildfires can burn through large land areas in just a few hours or days, damaging or destroying forests, grasslands, and anything else in their path. The damage can be staggering. When trees, bushes, and grasslands burn, entire habitats can be destroyed or damaged. When habitats are destroyed, it can take decades or even centuries for them to fully recover, if they ever do. Animals that are unable to escape the flames will die in the fire.

Others that manage to survive will struggle to find shelter or food afterward.

In Australia, historic wildfires burned from June 2019 to February 2020. Years of drought made the Australian bush very dry, which caused the destructive wildfires to burn for months. The fires burned over 27 million acres (11 million ha) across Australia's Southeastern region. Thousands of buildings were destroyed, and dozens of human lives were lost. The wildfires also killed or displaced nearly 3 billion animals, according to a World Wildlife Fund report. "It's a difficult number to comprehend,"[20] says Chris Dickman, professor of ecology at the University of Sydney. The damage was so widespread that some species previously unknown to scientists were likely lost in the fires. "We don't even know what we are losing," says Dickman. "These were species that were here, and now they have gone. . . . It's almost too tragic to think about."[21]

Endangered species are even more vulnerable to the damage caused by wildfires. The loss of critical habitats may irreparably damage their ability to survive and reproduce. The 2025 wildfires in California significantly damaged the habitats of several endangered species. "Critical coastal habitat, mountain habitat of California, has been scorched. There are endangered species, including California condors, mountain lions, black bears. There are many creatures now that, if they have not died in these fires, they have been displaced," says conservationist Jeff Corwin. Corwin explained that there were only about 350 California condors alive before the fires, making it a critically endangered species. "A significant piece of that population lives in ground zero of where these fires have happened,"[22] Corwin says. Time will tell how the fires ultimately impact California's endangered animals.

Soil Damage

Soil is an essential part of ecosystems. It is a natural filter for water and provides nutrients for growing plants. Soil supports many organisms that contribute to an ecosystem's biodiversity.

The California condor is just one endangered species threatened by wildfires.

Wildfires affect the soil, causing changes in structure, composition, and function.

Some damages to the soil make it harder for new plants to grow. For example, when wildfires increase soil temperatures significantly, the organic matter in the soil may burn. Decomposing organic matter is an important part of soil because it releases nutrients that plants use to grow. Organic matter also improves soil structure, which allows the soil to retain water and allows plant roots to grow. When wildfires burn the organic matter in soil, it changes the soil's ability to hold water and provide nutrients, which impacts the type of plants that can grow back after the fire.

Sometimes, the intense heat from a slow-moving wildfire can create a water-repellent layer in soil. As the fire burns vegetation, it creates a gas that enters the heated soil. As the soil cools, the gas condenses. It forms a waxy coating that makes the soil repel water instead of absorbing it. This phenomenon is known as hydrophobicity. When soil repels water, it increases the rate of water runoff. Less water in the soil also makes it more difficult for seeds to germinate and for plant roots to get the water they need to survive.

The ash produced when fires burn vegetation can initially deposit nutrients like nitrogen and phosphorus into the soil. However, these nutrients are deposited on the soil surface and can quickly be washed away by rain or erosion. The resulting nutrient-poor soil can impact soil fertility and the ability of plants to regrow. The intense heat from wildfires can also disrupt the microbes that live in the soil. Microbes are an essential part of decomposing organic material and returning nutrients into the soil. When the microbe community is disrupted by fire, the soil may become less able to support new plant growth.

Erosion

Other times, the damage from wildfires can increase the risk of soil erosion. Soil that is dried out and less able to absorb water after a wildfire has a greater risk of erosion. Erosion risk also increases because wildfires kill the trees and shrubs whose roots help anchor the soil in place. Without these roots, heavy rains can easily wash away topsoil, the fertile layer of soil needed for plant regrowth.

In some areas, erosion can trigger dangerous landslides, mudslides, or debris flows after a fire. Areas that have been charred and stripped of vegetation by a wildfire, known as burn scars, are particularly at risk. Heavy rains after a wildfire can trigger these mudslides for years after the fire. "The houses that are in the burn scar after a fire event are the most prone, most susceptible to there being a mudslide or debris flow around them,"[23] says Adam VanGerpen, a Los Angeles Fire Department captain.

"The houses that are in the burn scar after a fire event are the most prone, most susceptible to there being a mudslide or debris flow around them."[23]

—Adam VanGerpen, a Los Angeles Fire Department captain

Firefighting Costs

Fighting wildfires is expensive. Firefighters use specialized equipment, airplanes, and helicopters for water drops, and sometimes even military support. The longer and larger a fire is, the more resources are needed to contain it. Governments spend billions of dollars every year battling wildfires. In the United States the federal government spent more than $3 billion in 2023 on fire-suppression efforts. These costs are projected to increase in the coming years as wildfires become larger and more intense. States and local governments also spend money on fire prevention, emergency response, and rebuilding efforts.

In January 2025, sixty-three-year-old Stephen Edwards experienced firsthand the danger and destruction of both wildfires and a resulting landslide. First, Edwards lost his Pacific Palisades home in a massive wildfire. Despite the devastating loss, Edwards thought himself lucky because he had a second home, a rental property, that survived the blaze. Then a landslide drove his neighbor's house into his second home, causing the structure to split into two. Within a matter of weeks, Edwards lost two homes.

According to Farshid Vahedifard, an engineering professor at Tufts University, many parts of Southern California, like where Edwards lived, have deep slopes with loose soil, which increases landslide risk. The landscape, combined with the wildfire and the massive amounts of water used by firefighters to battle the huge blazes, created the conditions for a landslide. "These conditions make the area prone to landslides and debris flows, particularly when you have external triggers like wildfires,"[24] he says.

Air Pollution

As wildfires burn, they release large amounts of smoke into the air. Smoke pollution from smaller wildfires tends to stay close to the area burning. However, massive wildfires in areas like California and Canada have much more energy to push the smoke high into the atmosphere, where winds carry it farther away from the original blaze. In June 2025 smoke from nearly two hundred Canadian wildfires drifted south into the United States. People in parts of the US Midwest, including Minnesota, Wisconsin, and Michigan, were warned of very unhealthy levels of smoke pollution. The Canadian fires were so large that some of the smoke reached as far as Europe, causing hazy skies. "That's really an indicator of how intense these fires are, that they can deliver smoke [that far],"[25] says Mark Parrington, a senior scientist at the European climate service Copernicus.

Wildfire smoke is a mixture of gases, microscopic particles, and water vapor. The most significant air pollutant in wildfire smoke is microscopic particulate matter, a mixture of solid particles and liquid droplets. The composition of the particulate matter varies according to what is burning. "When you have trees burning, you have particles produced along with rapid volatilization [transformation into a gas] of the oils in the trees. When you have homes or other buildings burning, you also have emissions from burning different types of home materials, such as household cleaners, plastics, and finishes. The mix of hazardous toxins

People in New York City wear masks to protect themselves from Canadian wildfire smoke in June 2025. Wildfire smoke can travel a long distance and is harmful to health.

in the air is hard to predict,"[26] says Jennifer Richmond-Bryant, an associate professor of forestry and environmental resources at North Carolina State University.

The airborne particles in smoke are extremely small, typically less than 2.5 micrometers in diameter. That is about 1/70th of the size of a human hair. These particles can cause severe health problems, from eye irritation to respiratory distress. When inhaled, the particles can settle deep in a person's lungs or even enter the bloodstream. In some cases air pollution during a wildfire can be so bad that it is dangerous to go outside.

Flooding and Water Pollution

Large wildfires burn forests and vegetation and reduce the ability of soils to absorb water. The fires also destroy trees and vegetation that naturally absorb rainfall and reduce runoff. As a result of these changes, water runoff increases, especially after heavy rains. The runoff can cause flash flooding in some areas. It can also contaminate important water sources.

After a wildfire, water runoff carries ash, sediment, heavy metals, and other toxins from burned areas into rivers, streams, lakes, and reservoirs. When these chemicals and debris enter rivers and lakes, they can harm fish and other aquatic life. Drinking water can be contaminated, making it unsafe for people and animals.

In the summer of 2022, a massive Calf Canyon/Hermits Peak wildfire in New Mexico burned more than 300,000 acres (121,406 ha) of land. The flames came within 1 mile (1.6 km) of the small New Mexican town of Las Vegas, but firefighters were able to save the town from burning. Months later, however, heavy rains fell across the region and flooded the town. Residents scrambled to set up sandbags to protect their homes, and four people died in the flash floods.

The heavy rains also washed soot and ash left from the wildfire into the town's drinking water supplies. The town's water filtration system was overwhelmed by ashy sludge, causing a water shortage for residents. "First it was drought, then the fire, then the floods, then the water shortage," says Isaac Sandoval, a Las Vegas resident and restaurant owner. "What's next?"[27] To ease the water shortage, New Mexico installed a $2 million temporary pretreatment system. A permanent water treatment facility is estimated to cost between $100 million and $200 million.

> **"First it was drought, then the fire, then the floods, then the water shortage. What's next?"[27]**
>
> —Isaac Sandoval, a Las Vegas, New Mexico, resident who survived wildfire and related flash flooding

Andrew Whelton, a Purdue University engineering professor, has studied the impact of wildfires on drinking water. His research has found that several fires during 2017 to 2020 in Oregon and California contaminated drinking water for hundreds of thousands of people. Whelton warns that as wildfires increase in frequency and intensity, communities should prepare to protect their water supplies. "With the wildfires happening out West, no utility should be out there thinking that it's not going to happen to them,"[28] he said in 2022.

Economic Damage

The costs of wildfires go far beyond the burned trees and charred ground. Wildfires can have a major impact on local and national economies, destroying property, raising firefighting expenses, and hurting valuable industries such as farming, forestry, and tourism. A 2023 analysis from the US Congress Joint Economic Committee found that the total cost of wildfires in the United States is $394 billion to $893 billion annually. This amount includes the cost of property damage, deaths and injuries, health impacts from wildfire smoke, income loss, watershed pollution, and several additional factors.

It is easy to see the most immediate economic damage caused by wildfire along its burned path. Wildfires can burn homes, businesses, schools, and other structures to the ground in only a few hours. When a wildfire spreads through a town or neighborhood, it can leave hundreds or even thousands of people homeless. For example, the deadly 2025 Eaton and Palisades fires in California

Release of Carbon Dioxide

Burning wildfires release massive amounts of carbon dioxide into the atmosphere. As forests burn, the carbon stored in trees and plants is released. This creates a dangerous cycle. As more carbon dioxide builds up in the atmosphere, the earth's surface warms. Warming temperatures dry out vegetation and create conditions that lead to more fires. The cycle continues as the new fires release more carbon dioxide. A 2022 analysis found that the carbon dioxide released by California's wildfires might be erasing any gains the state's residents have made in reducing greenhouse gas (GHG) emissions. The study found that carbon emissions from California's 2020 fire season made up 30 percent of the state's greenhouse gas emissions. Says Michael Jerrett, study author and professor of environmental health sciences at the University of California, Los Angeles:

> To the great credit of California's policy-makers and residents, from 2003 to 2019, California's GHG emissions declined by 65 million metric tons of pollutants, a 13 percent drop that was largely driven by reductions from the electric power generation sector. Essentially, the positive impact of all that hard work over almost two decades is at risk of being swept aside by the smoke produced in a single year of record-breaking wildfires.

Quoted in Energy Policy Institute, University of Chicago, "Wildfires Are Erasing California's Climate Gains." October 17, 2022. www.epic.uchicago.edu.

destroyed or damaged more than eighteen thousand structures. Thousands of people were left homeless.

In addition to property losses, the 2025 Southern California wildfires damaged roads, bridges, power lines, and sewage systems, all of which needed repairs. Additionally, the affected communities incurred significant environmental and cleanup costs. Economic experts from the UCLA Anderson School of Management estimated that total property and capital losses from the wildfires could reach $76 billion to $131 billion.

Rebuilding homes, businesses, and communities is expensive and takes time. Families may be forced to move, businesses may close permanently, and it may take years for communities to recover. Insurance companies often pay out large amounts of money to cover losses, which can raise insurance premiums for everyone, no matter where they live.

Impact on Economic Activity

Wildfires disrupt economic activity by destroying physical infrastructure and disrupting transportation networks, making it difficult for people to work. Some industries in particular feel the effects of wildfires. The forestry industry loses valuable timber when trees are burned. As a result, logging companies may have to close, which can impact jobs.

When fires burn across farmland, they destroy crops, barns, and farming equipment. Livestock may be injured or killed. After the fire, the soil may be contaminated and unable to grow new crops for several years.

The tourism and recreation industries also suffer after wildfires. National parks, hiking trails, and other destinations are forced to close during and after wildfires. Lingering smoke and poor air quality can also cause tourists to stay away. When fewer people visit these places, local service businesses such as hotels, restaurants, and shops also lose money.

In Hawaii tourism is the state's largest industry. After the Maui wildfires in August 2023, the number of tourists dropped by 70 percent on Maui. For people like Richie Olsten, who operates a helicopter tour business in Maui, the drop in tourism has been devastating. Before the fires, Olsten's company operated about twenty-five to thirty flights a day. In September 2023 his company only flew about one or two flights daily. "I know what a terrible disaster that was," Olsten says about the wildfires. "But now we're in crisis mode. If we can't keep the people that have jobs employed, how are they going to help family members and friends that lost everything?"[29] Economists estimate that by one year later, Hawaii had lost nearly $1 billion in tourism revenue.

Health and Community Impacts

Wildfires do more than damage the environment and the economy. These blazes have a real impact on human health and communities. Fires threaten lives, cause significant health

Wildfire smoke can travel deep into a person's lungs, causing asthma attacks or other respiratory effects.

problems, and lead to long and difficult recoveries for affected communities.

Wildfires can quickly grow out of control. While firefighters and emergency responders put their lives at risk to save people, sometimes fires move too fast. People become trapped in their homes or cars with no way to escape in time. In recent years some of the deadliest wildfires have claimed dozens of lives. The 2023 Maui wildfire killed 102 people, making it the deadliest wildfire in the United States since 1900.

Even those who survive the flames can experience health problems. Tiny toxic particles in the fire's smoke can travel hundreds of miles and stay in the air for days. Breathing in this polluted air can cause coughing, headaches, chest pain, and other symptoms, especially for children and older people.

When inhaled, the microscopic particles in wildfire smoke can travel deep into a person's lungs. Some may even be small enough to pass through the lung membranes and enter the bloodstream. These particles can be especially dangerous for people who already have respiratory problems or heart disease. "When you're exposed to high quantities of particulate matter, even in a short period of time, it can lead to stroke or cardiac arrest. People may also have asthma attacks or other respiratory effects. It can also irritate the eyes and the skin,"[30] says Jennifer Richmond-Bryant.

Wildfires also take a toll on mental health. People who lose their homes or loved ones may suffer from anxiety, depression, or post-traumatic stress disorder (PTSD). The fear of future fires and the stress of evacuation and rebuilding can cause significant anxiety that lasts long after the fire is put out.

> **"When you're exposed to high quantities of particulate matter, even in a short period of time, it can lead to stroke or cardiac arrest. People may also have asthma attacks or other respiratory effects."[30]**
>
> —Jennifer Richmond-Bryant, associate professor of forestry and environmental resources at North Carolina State University

Researchers from the University of California, San Diego (UCSD), and California State University, Chico, studied the mental health impacts of the 2018 Camp Fire, a deadly and destructive event. They found that direct exposure to large-scale fires significantly increases a person's risk of developing a mental health disorder, especially PTSD and depression. In their study, the researchers found that people who had been exposed to the fire were three times more likely to have PTSD than the general population. "We see a very hyper-aroused brain system, which tends to happen when one feels like they're in constant threat mode. In this traumatic state, it makes it very difficult to go about day-to-day things in an attentive and focused way," says Jyoti Mishra, study coauthor and associate professor in the Department of Psychiatry at the UCSD School of Medicine. "We're still observing these brain responses six months to a year after the wildfires, which means there are longer-term impacts on this population,"[31] she adds.

The rising number of large, destructive wildfires worldwide has significant and long-lasting consequences. Wildfires destroy ecosystems and habitats, pollute the air and water, and cause billions of dollars in damage. Wildfires threaten human lives and health and leave behind people and communities struggling to recover. As the threat of wildfires increases, it is essential for communities worldwide to understand the serious impact they have and take steps to minimize risk before it is too late.

CHAPTER FOUR

How Are Communities Adapting?

In December 2021 Boulder County, Colorado, experienced the most destructive wildfire in the state's history. The fire ignited in a grassy area near the town of Marshall. A hot, dry summer and fall created an abundance of dry grass to fuel the fire, and strong winds spread the flames quickly. The wildfire destroyed over one thousand homes in Boulder County and caused approximately $500 million in damages. The amount of destruction in the affected communities was beyond anything previously experienced.

Several characteristics of the affected towns made them more vulnerable to fire. Drainage ditches built for flood control contained dry vegetation that fueled the fire and provided a highway for flames to spread. Open spaces and grasslands designed for community recreation and flood control enabled the fire to spread faster, burn more intensely, and move deeper within the towns.

Once the fire reached neighborhoods, flammable building materials, such as wooden roof shingles and vinyl siding, allowed flames to easily spread from house to house, quickly destroying entire neighborhoods. "You can almost think of it as a domino effect,"[32] says Michael Gollner, an associate professor at the University of California, Berkeley, Fire Research Lab. As soon as one house ignited in the Boulder County neighborhoods, the flames or burning embers it produced caused the neighbor's house to ignite, which ignited the next house on the street. One by one, houses all down the street burned. Dense vegetation close to homes provided more fire fuel and added to the damages.

Taking the lessons learned from the Marshall Fire and other destructive wildfires, many communities in fire-prone areas are taking action to minimize fire risk. Communities are changing how they plan and build neighborhoods, manage land, and use technology. They are implementing new fire safety policies and educating the public about wildfires and prevention plans. These efforts can help communities reduce the risks and impacts of wildfires.

Building Fire-Resistant Homes

Some communities are changing how they design and build homes and plan neighborhoods to minimize damage from a wildfire. Research shows that most homes and other structures ignite in a fire when a burning ember carried by wind lands on the home. Therefore, building and renovating homes with fire-resistant materials can limit fire spread and protect homes.

A home's roof is one of its most vulnerable areas in a wildfire. Burning embers will most likely land on the roof's large surface area. Roofs with wood shingles or some types of asphalt shingles are most flammable. Embers can also ignite debris on the roof or in gutters and can even enter the home through vents. Installing fire-resistant shingles or a metal roof and sealing vents can help protect the home against fire. Other modifications include replacing flammable vinyl siding with stucco, brick, or fiber-cement siding. Double-paned glass windows in fire-resistant frames can better withstand flying embers and the fire's heat than single-pane windows. Building decks and fences with fire-resistant materials instead of wood can also make a home more fire resistant.

Creating Space

The landscaping around homes and buildings also creates a fire risk. If the vegetation ignites, the flames can quickly spread to the home. Therefore, creating defensible space around properties is

In Ashland, Oregon, a crew removes dead trees and shrubs to make the community—which is in a high-risk fire zone—more fire resistant.

an essential part of reducing fire risk. Clearing away dead plants and dry leaves within 30 feet (9 m) of a home creates a buffer zone around the property that can slow or stop the spread of a fire by removing potential fuel. If there is nothing to burn, it will be difficult for the fire to intensify and spread.

Using hardscaping elements such as gravel or stone and fire-resistant plants in landscaping also reduces fire risk. Plants with thick leaves, a high moisture content, and a low resin content—such as succulents, yucca, and some species of lavender and lilac—are considered fire resistant. "Vegetation that tends to retain water and not dry easily and, at the same time, does not produce liquids, such as flammable oils and resin, should be considered. At the same time, it should be kept to a minimum and as far as possible from the main structure, preferably along the fence,"[33] says Fokion Egolfopoulos, a professor of engineering at the University of Southern California.

In Ashland, Oregon, residents are working to make their community, which is located in a high-risk fire zone, more fire resistant. In 2021 the Federal Emergency Management Agency awarded a $3 million grant to the city to help residents make changes to become more fire resistant. "This money is helping us reduce flammable landscaping in yards, and we're using these funds to work on and around 1,100 previously identified, at-risk homes. On the most vulnerable of these homes, we're working to replace outdated, wooden roofing,"[34] says Chris Chambers, the Ashland Fire & Rescue Department's wildfire division chief.

In southwestern Colorado, wildfires regularly threaten the forests near the town of Durango. The local nonprofit Wildfire Adapted Partnership (WAP) has brought in a team of fire safety experts to help residents make changes to protect their properties. WAP's team of ambassadors goes from neighborhood to neighborhood, helping residents learn how to make changes that will help reduce fire risk. Their efforts are working. The residents of one neighborhood north of Durango embraced WAP's recommendations. Community volunteers regularly perform fire-mitigation work such as thinning, trimming, and clearing brush, removing dead trees, and making their homes more fire resistant. Their mitigation efforts paid off when a wildfire approached the neighborhood in 2018. "As the fire moved into that area, what we found is that the mitigation work did what it was supposed to do. We were able to save every single structure in that area,"[35] says Chief Hal Doughty with the Durango Fire Department.

> "As the fire moved into that area, what we found is that the mitigation work did what it was supposed to do. We were able to save every single structure in that area."[35]
>
> —Hal Doughty, fire chief of Durango Fire Department

Policies and Regulations

In some fire-prone communities, local officials have created zoning regulations and development plans to minimize fire risk. These regulations require space between buildings and space between buildings and vegetation. They can limit building too close to for-

Datacasting

Communication is critical during a natural disaster, yet communication systems often fail or become overloaded during a catastrophic fire. The US federal government is exploring the use of datacasting, or using broadcast signals from digital television, to send critical data to firefighters and first responders during a wildfire. Datacasting is a reliable communications channel, particularly when traditional cellular networks may go down during a wildfire. Datacasting enables sending critical real-time data, such as where a fire perimeter is, hot spots, and other essential information to firefighters and other first responders. With this information, firefighters can make better decisions about how and where to send resources, predict how a fire will behave, and plan how to safely evacuate people. Datacasting allows officials to reach more people and share critical information fast.

ests or other areas where fires spread quickly. Incentives like tax breaks or rebates can also encourage people to take action and make their properties more fire resistant.

California has some of the country's strictest fire regulations. Since 2006 the state has required homeowners in high-risk areas to clear flammable materials within 100 feet (30.5 m) of structures. After the 2025 fires, Governor Gavin Newsom ordered the state to fast-track new regulations to create a new ember-resistant area, known as the "zone zero," around homes located in high-risk areas. The regulation aims to clear all materials that could ignite from flying embers carried by the wind. It bans items such as brush, wooden fencing, furniture, sheds, and mulch within 5 feet (1.5 meters) of homes. "We are living in a new reality of extremes. . . . Mother Nature is changing the way we live, and we must continue adapting to those changes. California's resilience means we will keep updating our standards in the most fire-prone areas,"[36] says Newsom.

"We are living in a new reality of extremes. . . . Mother Nature is changing the way we live, and we must continue adapting to those changes."[36]

—Gavin Newsom, governor of California

Paradise Rebuilds

In 2018 the town of Paradise, California, lost 90 percent of its homes in the massive Camp Fire. In the years after the fire, the town has slowly rebuilt. The rebuilding efforts have made fire safety a top priority. Paradise officials passed building regulations that require some of the strictest fire-resistant standards in the United States. "It was really important to us that we learned lessons from what happened here and that we share those, but we're really looking at the science that exists now to make it better here,"[37] says Colette Curtis, the town's recovery coordinator.

Now in Paradise, all new homes are built with fire-resistant materials and include ember-resistant venting and metal gutters. Properties must also maintain a mandatory 5 feet (1.5 m) of defensible space around the home and a 6-foot (1.8 m) vertical clearance above all exterior walls to prevent flammable material from getting too close to the home. Residents can still build a fence around their property, but if it lies within the 5-foot buffer, it must be made of noncombustible materials. During the Camp Fire, many wood fences ignited and spread the fire to nearby homes.

To help the town's rebuilding, the Rebuild Paradise Foundation provides fire-wise design plans and grants to residents to help them build fire-resistant homes. Says Jenni Goodlin, executive director of the foundation:

> The idea is, if we are building back, let's manage it better this time, right? We have a new start, so let's start with, right after we build the home, let's provide homeowners with gravel, so that they have 5 feet of defensible space right out the gate. Versus someone just planting trees and not knowing or not understanding.[38]

Paradise has also taken steps to protect the community beyond building fire-resistant homes. Outside Paradise, hundreds of thousands of trees have been removed to slow and reduce the intensity of an approaching fire before it reaches the town. Power lines have been run underground within the town to prevent sparks that could accidentally ignite a fire. During the Camp Fire, some people died as they tried to evacuate in their cars. Now

Paradise has widened and redesigned roads to make evacuating easier if another fire threatens the town. "So we're building the houses but also the town. We're rebuilding the town in a way to be able to withstand something as catastrophic as the Camp Fire if it were to happen 100 years from now,"[39] says Ron Lossande, a former mayor of Paradise.

Forest Management

Years of fire suppression and poor forest management have led to many forests being overgrown, weakened from disease, and filled with dry or dead trees, brush, and other vegetation. These materials fuel wildfires, helping them grow faster and more intensely. Some communities are managing dense and overgrown forests with controlled burns. A controlled burn is a small, planned fire that is set intentionally under safe conditions. A controlled burn burns away dry, dead plants before they can fuel wildfires. Other forest management practices—such as thinning forests, removing dead trees, and clearing excessive underbrush—also help reduce

A controlled burn is a small, planned fire that is intentionally set in order to burn away dry, dead plants before they can fuel wildfires.

the amount of fuel available for future wildfires. By reducing fire fuel with active forest management practices, communities hope future wildfires will be slower, less intense, and easier to control.

At the University of California, Berkeley, researchers have studied the impact of active forest management practices in the Sierra Nevada for more than twenty years. The study's results, published in 2023, found that active forest management techniques—including controlled burning, restoration thinning, or a combination of both—were all effective at reducing the risk of catastrophic wildfires. Researchers noted that these forest management practices also improved overall forest health. Trees were more resilient to drought and insects, while plants and wildlife biodiversity did not suffer. "The research is pretty darn clear that these treatments are effective—very effective," says study lead author Scott Stephens, a professor of fire science at the University of California, Berkeley. "I hope this lets people know that there is great hope in doing these treatments at scale, without any negative consequences."[40]

The idea of controlled burning is not new. For thousands of years, many Indigenous peoples used a form of controlled burning known as cultural burning to manage the land where they

The Importance of Public Education

Public education is an essential part of wildfire adaptation and can save lives. Many communities now hold campaigns to teach people about fire prevention and safety. These campaigns might include posters, videos, classroom lessons, and community events. In Durango, Colorado, for example, local officials work with schools and neighborhoods to raise awareness. They organize community drills where people practice what to do if a wildfire threatens their area. These drills can include checking emergency kits, planning evacuation routes, and making sure everyone knows where to go. Education also helps people understand what causes wildfires and how to prevent them. For example, teaching people not to leave campfires unattended or throw cigarette butts into dry grass can prevent many fires from starting. In some areas programs teach homeowners how to create defensible space and choose fire-safe plants for landscaping. Emergency planning is another focus of wildfire education. Families are encouraged to make emergency plans and keep supplies like water, food, flashlights, and masks in case they need to evacuate quickly. Knowing ahead of time what to do makes people calmer and more prepared when a wildfire threatens.

lived and minimize wildfire risk. These small fires were used to clear brush, promote plant growth, and prevent larger wildfires. Research from the University of California, Berkeley, found that forest biomass, or organic plant matter, in the Klamath Mountains used to be about half of its current level. Cultural burns by the Karuk and Yurok people had a significant role in shaping the forests. Yet European settlers viewed the practice as primitive and outlawed it.

Now some experts recognize the benefit of cultural burning practices and are working with Indigenous groups to bring them back. A 2022 California law affirmed the right to cultural burns. A 2019 study, led by Stanford University researchers in collaboration with the US Forest Service and the Yurok and Karuk tribes, proposed expanding cultural burns across more than 1 million acres (404,686 ha) of federal and tribal lands. Says Lenya N. Quinn-Davidson, Northern California Prescribed Fire Council director:

> There is so much to learn from cultural practitioners—not just about traditions and techniques, but also about stewardship and connectedness. Fire is a reflection of culture, and the kinds of fires we've been experiencing in California are a projection of our own disconnection and imbalance. It's time to reclaim the balance, rebuild the relationship. Cultural practitioners can help show us how.[41]

Technology and Early Warning Systems

Technology is also playing a role in helping communities adapt to wildfires. New tools can help predict fires before they start, detect fires early, predict how they will spread, and warn people in time to act. Remote sensing technologies such as satellite images, drones, and airborne sensors can scan large areas and help people assess current conditions. Remote sensors can detect changes in moisture levels, vegetation density, and temperature, which can increase the risk of wildfires. With this information, communities can set up controlled burns or work to clear risky vegetation to minimize fire risk before a blaze begins.

Once a fire starts, satellites and sensors take pictures and scan for signs of heat or smoke. Firefighters use this information to locate fires quickly and control them before they grow too big. Some communities are testing new wildfire sensors developed by the US Department of Homeland Security. Traditional sensors detect fires using cameras or thermal imaging. The new sensors can detect heat and smoke by analyzing the air for gases and airborne particulate levels common in wildfires. When the sensors detect air conditions that indicate a fire is burning, they send alerts to firefighters, allowing them to respond faster. The US Department of Homeland Security is currently testing the sensors in several states, including California, Colorado, Tennessee, and Arizona.

A drone is used to help improve fire safety. Technology like this can help communities adapt to wildfires.

Researchers are also developing artificial intelligence systems to predict where fires might start and how they will spread. At the University of Southern California (USC), researchers have developed an artificial intelligence model that uses satellite data to predict where wildfires will spread. The model takes satellite data to track a wildfire in real time and then feeds the data into algorithms that predict the fire's path, how intense it will become, and how fast it will grow. "This model represents an important step forward in our ability to combat wildfires. By offering more precise and timely data, our tool strengthens the efforts of firefighters and evacuation teams battling wildfires on the front lines,"[42] says Bryan Shaddy, a USC doctoral student and study coauthor.

> **"This model represents an important step forward in our ability to combat wildfires. By offering more precise and timely data, our tool strengthens the efforts of firefighters and evacuation teams battling wildfires on the front lines."[42]**
>
> —Bryan Shaddy, a doctoral student at the USC Viterbi School of Engineering

As wildfires grow more common and dangerous, communities are finding new and better ways to adapt. Fire-resilient planning, forest and land management, technology, and smart policies and regulations all have an important part in an overall strategy. Together, these strategies can help reduce the damage from wildfires and keep people, homes, and nature safer.

SOURCE NOTES

Introduction: Historic Devastation

1. Quoted in Gavin Feek, "Climbers, Hikers, and Runners Share Survival Stories from the Los Angeles Wildfires," *Outside*, January 13, 2025. www.outsideonline.com.
2. Quoted in Riley Hoffman et al., "LA Fires Aftermath: How People Are Rebuilding After Losing Almost Everything," ABC News, March 7, 2025. https://abcnews.go.com.
3. Quoted in Jacob Soboroff and Alexandra Marquez, "Newsom Says California Wildfires Will Be One of the Worst Natural Disasters in U.S. History," NBC News, January 12, 2025. www.nbcnews.com.
4. Quoted in University of Michigan News, "The Impact of Los Angeles Wildfires: U-M Experts Can Comment," January 9, 2025. https://news.umich.edu.

Chapter One: What Are Wildfires?

5. Quoted in Brian Perry, "Deadly Lahaina Fire Spread 'Incredibly Fast,' Racing Mauka to Makai Within 90 Minutes," Maui Now, April 18, 2023. www.mauinow.com.
6. Quoted in ABC7 Los Angeles, "'There's Just Nothing Left.' Maui Resident Jumped into Ocean to Escape Flames That Overtook His Home," August 11, 2023. www.abc7.com.
7. Quoted in Laura Paddison, "Why Do Arsonists Set Fires? The Reasons Are Sometimes Dark and Surprising," CNN, February 3, 2025. www.cnn.com.
8. Quoted in Andrew Moore, "Explainer: How Wildfires Start and Spread," College of Natural Resources News, December 3, 2021. https://cnr.ncsu.edu.
9. Quoted in Moore, "Explainer."
10. Quoted in Jeff Daniels, "Officials: Camp Fire, Deadliest in California History, Was Caused by PG&E Electrical Transmission Lines," CNBC, May 15, 2019. www.cnbc.com.

Chapter Two: Why Are Wildfires Increasing?

11. Quoted in Yale Sustainability, "Yale Experts Explain Wildfires," January 21, 2021. https://sustainability.yale.edu.

12. Quoted in University of Michigan News, "The Impact of Los Angeles Wildfires."
13. Quoted in Virginia Tech News, "Expert Shares Factors Increasing Forest Fire Ignitions," December 17, 2024. https://news.vt.edu.
14. Quoted in Theo Stein, "Study: Heat, Not Lack of Precipitation, Is Driving Western U.S. Droughts," NOAA Research, November 8, 2024. https://research.noaa.gov.
15. Quoted in Julie Cart, "Lightning Could Spark More California Fires as World Warms," CalMatters, September 24, 2021. https://calmatters.org.
16. Quoted in Yale Sustainability, "Yale Experts Explain Wildfires."
17. Quoted in Virginia Tech News, "Expert Shares Factors Increasing Forest Fire Ignitions."
18. Quoted in Warren Cornwall, "Flammable Invasive Grasses Are Increasing Risk of Devastating Wildfires," *Science*, August 4, 2022. www.science.org.
19. Quoted in Cornwall, "Flammable Invasive Grasses Are Increasing Risk of Devastating Wildfires."

Chapter Three: What Are the Consequences of More Frequent, Destructive Wildfires?

20. Quoted in Daniel Vernick, "3 Billion Animals Harmed by Australia's Fires," World Wildlife Fund, July 28, 2020. www.worldwildlife.org.
21. Quoted in Reuters, "About Three Billion Animals Harmed in Australian Bushfires, WWF Says," July 29, 2020. www.reuters.com.
22. Quoted in Angela Barbuti, "Endangered Species Threatened by LA Fires—and Missing Pets May Return to Properties After Flames Extinguished: Expert," *New York Post*, January 11, 2025. www.nypost.com.
23. Quoted in Randi Richardson et al., "Los Angeles Home Survived Fire, Only to Be Damaged by Landslide," NBC News. January 17, 2025. www.nbcnews.com.
24. Quoted in Richardson et al., "Los Angeles Home Survived Fire, Only to Be Damaged by Landslide."
25. Quoted in Associated Press, "Canadian Wildfire Smoke Causes 'Very Unhealthy' Conditions in American Midwest and Reaches Europe," WCCB Charlotte's CW, June 3, 2025. www.wccbcharlotte.com.
26. Quoted in Emma Gosalvez, "How Do Wildfires Impact Air Quality?," College of Natural Resources, September 14, 2020. https://cnr.ncsu.edu.

27. Quoted in Simon Romero, "How New Mexico's Largest Wildfire Set Off a Drinking Water Crisis," *New York Times*, September 26, 2022. www.nytimes.com.
28. Quoted in Romero, "How New Mexico's Largest Wildfire Set Off a Drinking Water Crisis."
29. Quoted in Audrey McAvoy and Jennifer Sinco Kelleher, "Maui Beckons Tourists, and Their Dollars, to Stave Off Economic Disaster After Wildfires," *AP News*, September 7, 2023. https://apnews.com.
30. Quoted in Gosalvez, "How Do Wildfires Impact Air Quality?"
31. Quoted in Malinda Danziger, "Wildfires Have a Lasting Psychological Impact on Communities," UC San Diego Today, May 1, 2024. https://today.ucsd.edu.

Chapter Four: How Are Communities Adapting?

32. Quoted in Elissaveta M. Brandon, "What It's Really Going to Take to Build Fire-Resistant Communities," *Fast Company*, February 2025. www.fastcompany.com.
33. Quoted in Marc Ballon, "Five Things You Can Do to Help Fireproof Your House," USC Viterbi School of Engineering, February 10, 2025. https://viterbischool.usc.edu.
34. Quoted in Nature Conservancy, "Local Communities Adapting to Fire," August 15, 2021. www.nature.org.
35. Quoted in Nature Conservancy, "Local Communities Adapting to Fire."
36. Quoted in Governor of California, "Governor Newsom Signs Executive Order to Further Prepare for Future Urban Firestorms, Stepping Up Already Nation-Leading Strategies," February 7, 2025. www.gov.ca.gov.
37. Quoted in Phillip Palmer, "7 on Your Side: 'Build Back Safer' Regulations Guide Paradise's Recovery 6 Years After Camp Fire," ABC7 Los Angeles, February 14, 2025. https://abc7.com.
38. Quoted in Palmer, "7 on Your Side."
39. Quoted in Palmer, "7 on Your Side."
40. Quoted in Kara Manke, "Twenty-Year Study Confirms California Forests Are Healthier When Burned—or Thinned," Berkeley News, December 12, 2023. https://news.berkeley.edu.
41. Quoted in Robyn Schelenz, "How the Indigenous Practice of 'Good Fire' Can Help Our Forests Thrive," University of California, April 6, 2022. www.universityofcalifornia.edu.
42. Quoted in David Medzerian, "Scientists Use AI to Predict a Wildfire's Next Move," USC Today, July 22, 2024. https://today.usc.edu.

FOR FURTHER RESEARCH

Books

Ferin Davis Anderson and Stephanie Sammartino McPherson, *Wildfire: The Culture, Science, and Future of Fire*. Twenty-First Century, 2024.

Heidi Fiedler and Smithsonian Institution, *Wildfires*. Teacher Created Materials, 2025.

Albert Marrin, *When Forests Burn: The Story of Wildfires in America*. Knopf, 2023.

Don Nardo, *Climate Change Impact: Wildfires*. ReferencePoint, 2025.

Jessica Stremer, *Fire Escape: How Animals and Plants Survive Wildfires*. Holiday House, 2024.

Internet Sources

CAL FIRE, "Wildfire Action Plan," 2025. https://readyforwildfire.org.

Andrew Moore, "Explainer: How Wildfires Start and Spread." College of Natural Resources News, December 3, 2021. https://cnr.ncsu.edu.

Andrew Moore, "How Do Wildfires Impact the Environment?," College of Natural Resources News, February 21, 2025. https://cnr.ncsu.edu.

National Geographic, "Wildfires: How They Form, and Why They're So Dangerous," October 19, 2023. https://education.nationalgeographic.org.

National Park Service, "Explore Fire in Depth," May 4, 2022. www.nps.gov.

Matthew Wibbenmeyer and Anne McDarris, "Wildfires in the United States 101: Context and Consequences," Resources for the Future, July 30, 2021. www.rff.org.

Organizations and Websites

Brookings Institution
www.brookings.edu
The Brookings Institution is a nonprofit public policy organization based in Washington, DC. It strives to conduct nonpartisan,

in-depth research on problems facing society at the local, national, and global levels. Its website features a section on climate that includes the latest articles, essays, research, reports, and more.

Cato Institute
www.cato.org
The Cato Institute is a public policy research organization that researches and promotes libertarian ideas in policy debates. Its website features information on a variety of issues, including numerous climate-related resources such as podcasts, research briefs, news articles, policy briefs, and more.

Federal Emergency Management Agency
www.fema.gov
The Federal Emergency Management Agency coordinates the federal government's response to disasters, including wildfires. Its website has a section focused on wildfire action that has information about grants, current fires, resources, and how to prepare for wildfires.

National Interagency Fire Center
www.nifc.gov
The National Interagency Fire Center brings together several federal and state agencies to provide support to wildland firefighting efforts. Its website features the latest news, information, and mitigation and preparedness resources for wildfires.

US Forest Service
www.fs.usda.gov
The US Forest Service is an agency within the US Department of Agriculture. It administers the country's national forests and grasslands. Its website has information about fire management, fire science, forest health, and more.

INDEX

PICTURE CREDITS

Cover: Paulo M. F. Pires/Shutterstock

5: Ringo Chiu/Shutterstock
9: Associated Press
12: John D Sirlin/Shutterstock
17: Maury Aaseng
21: Randy Beacham/Alamy
24: Cavan Images/Alamy
28: Klaus Reitmeier/Alamy
32: Escap/Shutterstock
35: lev radin/Shutterstock
40: antoniodiaz/Shutterstock
45: J.G. Domke/Alamy
49: Denis MacDonald/Shutterstock
52: valentyn Semenov/Shutterstock

ABOUT THE AUTHOR

Carla Mooney is the author of many books for young adults and children. She lives in Pittsburgh, Pennsylvania, with her husband and three children.